Faces of Law

PHOTOGRAPHS BY JAMES F. HUNKIN

Faces of Law

PHOTOGRAPHS BY JAMES F. HUNKIN

WILDY, SIMMONDS & HILL
PUBLISHING

Faces of Law

First published in 2008 by
Wildy, Simmonds & Hill Publishing Ltd
58 Carey Street, London WC2A 2JB, UK

British Library Cataloguing-in-Publication Data:
A catalogue record for this book is available from The British Library

ISBN 9780854900276

Designed and typeset by Oblong Creative Ltd, Wetherby, LS23 7BJ

Contents

Barristers

Judiciary

Others

Introduction

Faces of Law is the fifth in a series of on-going chronicles I have produced of the people of Britain at the turn of the twenty-first century. In this instance, I have tried to paint a representative picture of the legal community, which includes senior members of the judiciary, leaders in their various fields as well as respected figures and those working behind the front line.

It should come as no surprise, but still it surprises me, how different the characters are, their motivations and the actual jobs they do, whether it is within the glass palaces of the billion-dollar law firms, or the cloisters of the Inns of Court, the inner city law centres, or the Old Bailey, to name but a few.

Having successfully completed many years of study, lawyers can expect generous salaries, which can offer motivation enough, while others clearly revel in the intellectual challenge of getting to grips with multi-dimensional conflicts, clarifying the arguments and then bringing them to the public arena. Others see the law as a means to improve and protect the lives of people who have been subject to unfair treatment by the state. For some it is the human drama played out in moments of conflict that provides the buzz.

I was asked by a number of subjects why I was interested in photographing 'boring old lawyers'.

I hope that the photographs speak for themselves in response to their concern.

Alongside each photograph there is a short factual piece written by me, and some text, written or selected by the subject, that provides an insight into the work they do or that offers a personal perception of the role of law in society.

Acknowledgements

This collection would not have materialised without the support of numerous people.

As with all these collections I am indebted to the subjects themselves for agreeing to give up their valuable time, not only to be photographed but also to offer their written contributions.

In particular, I am indebted to the remarkable Baroness Hale whose interest in the project enabled me to secure a major sponsor. The Nuffield Foundation provided the necessary means for the project to achieve lift-off and I am very grateful for their continued support and interest.

Metro Imaging, Mayer Brown Rowe & Maw, and Marks & Clerk have been generous in their support, without which the collection would not have been completed. I would also like to thank Cliff Birtchnell for his generosity in allowing me to use his darkroom on numerous occasions.

I am forever in debt to my wife, Deborah, for believing in me and the project.

Lastly, I should also like to a say a special word of thanks to my Mother and Father who have encouraged me at every turn along a road with many twists and turns.

James F. Hunkin

Lawyers

John Balfour

Lawyer, Aviation

John Balfour practices in all areas of aviation law, with particular reference to EC law and regulatory law. He is a fellow of the Royal Aeronautical Society, a member of the International Advisory Board of the International Institute of Air & Space Law and expert adviser to NATO's Civil Aviation Planning Committee.

He has acted for IATA before the European Court of Justice, as well as various airlines including British Airways, Virgin, KLM, Air New Zealand and Lufthansa. John has conducted a number of studies for the European Commission, one of which dealt with airlines' conditions of carriage and the EC unfair terms directive, which led to the so-called "Balfour Report".

He has appeared before both Houses of Parliament giving evidence and advice on EC aviation matters.

I feel fortunate to work in such a fascinating area of law as air law. It involves most of the main areas of law, the international and political aspects are interesting, and the changes in the industry resulting from liberalisation and the increased role of the European Community give rise to novel legal issues and opportunities.

Joe Beltrami

Solicitor-Advocate

Following his qualification as a solicitor in 1954, Joe Beltrami has risen to become one of the best known and respected figures at the Scottish Bar. He has been instructed in twelve capital murder cases as well as hundreds of non-capital murder cases and gained the only two royal pardons granted in Scotland during the last century.

He is also a long-term sports enthusiast, having chaired the testimonials of senior Celtic and Rangers players over a number of years.

Yes, I have enjoyed my Law career, complete with the excitement and pleasures accompanying it, having often said that when the urge, interest, challenges and thrills disappear, then so shall I.

BELTRAMI &
Solicitors &
83

Raju Bhatt

Lawyer, Police Law

Raju Bhatt's practice over the last two decades has been shaped by his work with those who have suffered abuse of power or neglect of duty within the police and prison service, including families of those who have died in custody.

A major theme of Raju's work has concerned the requirement that those entrusted with upholding the rule of law should be seen to be accountable to the rule of law. The resulting focus of the work has inevitably fallen upon the conduct and quality of official investigations into allegations of wrongdoing and ensuing decision making processes whereby those responsible may be subject to criminal prosecutions or disciplinary proceedings.

Raju's considerable expertise and experience has been called upon many times by the CPS, Home Office, Independent Police Complaints Commission, Attorney General and Metropolitan Police.

My work with the law has been shaped by my clients and their endeavours to obtain some semblance of accountability and redress in respect of their experiences. They tend to be those who have endured abuse of power or neglect of duty on the part of the state and its officials, in particular within the police service and the prison service. From their point of view, notions of 'justice' often appear to be illusory. And yet, they tend to retain their dignity with their resilience, and their insistence that everyone should be equally answerable to the rule of law in the hope that others may be spared what they have had to suffer – that gives me the reason to come in to work everyday.

Nigel Boardman

Lawyer, Corporate

Nigel Boardman joined Slaughter & May, one of the so-called 'magic circle' City law firms, almost 35 years ago and has risen to become a venerated figure in the area of Mergers & Acquisitions, advising a remarkable twelve FTSE-100 companies.

He has been involved in many high profile mergers including recently, Asda and Wal-Mart, Orange and Mannesmann, the Astra-Zeneca merger, Shell's purchase of Enterprise Oil and has successfully defended Marks & Spencer against hostile acquisition on two occasions.

For me it's the perfect job – it's intellectually stimulating, you get to work with outstanding people, you can help the development of younger lawyers, it permits creativity; every day is different, it is never dull – and sometimes you even get to make a difference.

Ian Burton

Solicitor, Fraud

Fraud is a widespread and growing offence, estimated to cost the UK economy £14 billion a year. In response, the Government introduced the Fraud Act 2006, which set out a general offence of fraud replacing the previous patchwork of statutory crimes in English law to better equip police and prosecutors to deal with the challenge of combating fraud in the 21st century. Fraud is now defined in three ways: by false representation, by wrongfully failing to disclose information and by abuse of position.

Recently a man behind a £54m VAT fraud gang was sentenced to 15 years in prison – the longest ever UK sentence for such a crime.

In advising a client I find that it is the application of the law combined with a generous helping of common sense, a little sympathy and a touch of human kindness that is the best recipe for success.

Mark Campbell

Lawyer, Global Head of Finance

Mark Campbell works for Clifford Chance, the largest law firm in the world, both by number of lawyers and revenue, becoming the world's first billion-dollar business law firm (and the biggest-billing law firm ever) in 2006, registering record revenues of $2.039 billion.

In the same year, they topped three tables for worldwide M&A, advising on 444 deals globally which were valued at a total of $490 billion.

The firm also employs about 4,000 lawyers worldwide. It has twenty-seven offices spread across 20 countries in North and South America, Europe, the Middle East and Asia. The firm's London headquarters in Canary Wharf provides a range of round the clock amenities to its staff, including a gymnasium, swimming pool, squash courts and medical centre.

My job allows me to work with very bright and committed people – colleagues and clients. Over the years it has been the sense of being a part of that community which has been the most important part of the job for me.

Our clients ask us to structure and implement complex financial transactions, usually dealing with legal issues in numerous different countries. We get huge satisfaction from achieving what the clients ask us to do. Although the law has its own intellectual attractions, it is this practical aspect which continues to excite and interest me.

Shami Chakrabarti

Human Rights Lawyer and Campaigner

Also known as the National Council for Civil Liberties, Liberty was founded in 1934 at the heart of the movement for fundamental rights and freedoms in England and Wales.

Liberty campaigns to protect basic rights and freedoms through the courts, in Parliament and the wider community. They do this through a combination of public campaigning, test case litigation, parliamentary lobbying, policy analysis and the provision of free advice and information.

After graduating from the LSE, Shami Chakrabarti worked as a barrister at the Home Office before joining Liberty in 2001, and was subsequently appointed Director in September 2003. She is a prominent opponent of recent counter-terrorism legislation and is a frequent contributor to BBC Radio 4 and to *The Independent* newspaper on civil liberties.

'It was the boast of Augustus that he found Rome of brick and left it of marble. But how much nobler will be the sovereign's boast when he shall have it to say that he found law , , , a sealed book and left it a living letter; found it a patrimony of the rich and left it the inheritance of the poor; found it the two-edged sword of craft and oppression and left it the staff of honesty and the shield of innocence.'

HENRY BROUGHAM

David Cheyne

Corporate Lawyer, Senior Partner

Since joining a leading 'magic circle' law firm thirty years ago as an assistant solicitor, David Cheyne is now Senior Partner with the same firm generating a turnover in excess of £1 billion.

Has been involved in a wide range of corporate transactions including all types of mergers and acquisitions, joint ventures, flotations and general corporate finance work.

I wanted to be a banker when I started and qualified as a lawyer since I thought it would be a useful stepping stone. I thought that practising as a lawyer might be dull. I was wrong. There are few more interesting things to do than advising on a takeover – particularly if it is hostile. It is fun and it is never dull. You never stop having to think of new ways to do things. So I never did make the change.

Dorcas Crawford

Civil Litigation, NI

Dorcas studied law at Queen's University Belfast, graduating in 1987.

She has conducted a number of high profile and ground breaking cases, such as the application to the High Court in 2002 for an order permitting revolutionary treatment for Jonathan Simms, a vCJD sufferer. The application was successful and Jonathan received the treatment, making him the longest known survivor of the disease.

Recently, she has conducted the longest running civil action in Northern Ireland – a Group Action for 5,000 police officers for Post Traumatic Stress Disorder against their employer, the Chief Constable.

She has also recently received two appointments as solicitor to the NI Social Care Council, in relation to misconduct proceedings against social workers, and to the County Court Rules Committee.

For me being a lawyer is about doing something for people that they can't do for themselves – it's about giving them a voice when sometimes their own isn't loud enough, and if you ask my children they'll tell you that mine can be louder than most.

Alison Eddy

Lawyer, Clinical Negligence

Alison enjoys a national reputation as one of the leading solicitors in both clinical negligence and neurotrauma litigation.

Her particular area of expertise is in claims for those who have suffered brain injury and associated disability as a consequence of failings in medical care in both NHS and private hospitals. Her experience in these types of claims is extensive including claims arising from obstetric, neonatal, anaesthetic, neurosurgical, cardiac and emergency care. She also represents clients who have suffered serious injury as the result of traffic accidents.

Alison lectures regularly to other lawyers and health care professionals on clinical negligence litigation and personal injury related topics. She has contributed a number of articles to journals dealing particularly with consent issues.

I hear heartbreaking stories of loss and see the terrible impact on the wider family when a child or partner suffers a devastating injury.

What motivates me is knowing I can make a real difference to the lives of my clients, particularly through the process of rehabilitation. I care passionately that they are properly compensated for the injury they have suffered as the result of a medical accident or, often quite senseless, road traffic accident.

I can think of nothing I would rather do.

Steve Edge

Lawyer, Tax

Since qualifying in 1975, Steve Edge has for many years been a leading practitioner in tax law as it relates to corporate finance, including leasing, securitisations and complex financial instruments.

He acts for a wide range of clients, advising on tax structuring and the tax aspects of documenting both private and public mergers, acquisitions, disposals and joint ventures. He acts for investment banks in relation to their structured finance businesses and advises non-UK multinationals, particularly those based in the US, on cross-border transactions of various types.

He is also currently an advisor to the government on tax related issues.

Nobody believes me when I say tax has been a lot of fun – but it has.

Charlie Geffen

Lawyer, Private Equity

Charlie Geffen studied law at Leicester University and is one of the leading lawyers advising private equity firms. His law firm has approximately 800 lawyers and 13 offices around the world and is one of the leading law firms representing some of the best known private equity houses and lending banks.

He joined the firm as a trainee in 1982, becoming a partner in 1991. He heads the firm's private equity practice and is a member of the firm's Board. Charlie has led teams on some of the best known private equity deals including Merlin Entertainments and Madame Tussauds, Gala Coral, Center Parcs, Legoland and National Car Parks.

Private equity firms are financial investors who acquire businesses with a combination of their own money and bank borrowing. They manage those businesses for a number of years growing them either organically or by acquisition with a view to selling them or floating them on the public market.

Academic cleverness is not a prerequisite – indeed it can be a hindrance.

Nipun Gupta

Lawyer, M&A

Nipun Gupta is a Partner at an international law firm in the City of London and the driving force behind their India practice. Prior to that she was head of legal at MittalSteel, the world's largest steel-making group. She advises international clients on mergers and acquisitions with a particular focus on emerging markets.

She is a mentor for the Prince's Trust and a member of the India Business Group and Infrastructure and Finance Committee at the Indian High Commission as well as being a member of the Asian Business Panel at The Bank of England.

Nipun recently received a prestigious Law Day award from the Indian Prime Minister to acknowledge her position as a "role model for women lawyers in India and abroad". The National Law Day Awards are given in recognition of outstanding contributions in the field of law.

The good news is it is possible to pursue and achieve success and excitement and conduct oneself with integrity at the same time – you just have to work a little harder for it.

"Whatever happened was good, whatever is happening is good, whatever will happen will also be good. Change is the law of the Universe."

GEETA SAAR

Mark Haslam

Lawyer, Crime

Criminal law, as opposed to civil law which rights wrongs done to individuals, is concerned with public order and the common good. In earlier times when the notion of a 'state' was not so strong, this distinction was not always so clear. Criminal acts were deemed to be acts against the individual which were then settled by the victim's family, and the emergence of a separate strand of criminal law emerged in order to protect the perpetrator from excessive revenge rather than from any desire to punish.

Today, less serious crimes, such as motoring offences and public disturbance, are heard at Magistrates courts with the more serious cases heard before a jury at a Crown Court. The most sensitive cases are presided over by High Court Judges, with the Court of Appeal reserved for cases where a point of law is called in to question.

In my second year at university whilst studying for my law degree, I took an optional course in Criminology and from that moment onwards, decided that if I was to stay in law, it would be in the field of criminal law.

I regard myself as extremely fortunate in having had the opportunity to practice in this field which I find challenging, satisfying and enjoyable even now after 26 years in practice and can confidently say that if I had the opportunity to make my career decision again I would make exactly the same decision.

Tim Hellier

Lawyer, Planning

The inherent conflicts between those wanting to utilise land for commercial or residential purposes and those seeking to protect and maintain the existing natural environment has never been higher on the political agenda.

Planning laws govern how we live through the decisions that are made relating to transport and housing as well as protecting the environment and our heritage.

Tim Hellier's practice includes concept development and strategic direction, planning inquiries, reviews on planning and infrastructure prior to purchase and negotiating with Local Authorities. His particular areas of expertise include High Court planning actions, town centre redevelopment and large-scale urban regeneration projects.

Planning law is one of the most diverse areas of specialist legal practice. There is perhaps a surprising amount of legal content emanating for the statutory code, judicial review and European legislation, and part of our task is keeping major planning applications out of the clutches of the Secretary of State and the Courts. But it is much more than this. Lawyers are at the heart of development projects where Law and policy (on an ever changing canvas!) shapes projects and the environments they create.

Graham Huntley

Lawyer, Litigation

When disputes arise between two or more parties, litigation may be called upon as a precursor to the trial proper, in order to set out the terms of the dispute as well as opening up the possibility for dispute resolution as a more cost-effective way of resolving the issues.

The litigator will make an analysis of the client's case, thereby assisting the client to recognise the pertinent issues and make a realistic assessment of the other side's position. In the event of a case going to trial or hearing, he will advise a barrister and assist him in the presentation of the case acting as intermediary between solicitor and barrister. He will also advise on "out of court" settlements.

Graham has been a partner since 1993 focusing on disputes involving banks and large corporates with a particular emphasis on City related problems such as M&A disputes, fund and asset management disputes, as well as shareholder and joint venture disputes.

The large international law firms will come to dominate the legal world. Despite their increasing complexity it is important that we all recognise that the business is built on some simple principles. At the core is commitment to client service, but we cannot forget the need for communities like these to operate to a common purpose and standard which can create an exacting management agenda. No one should pretend that it is easy, but the challenge of getting it right internationally, whilst never forgetting the commitment to the client on the ground, creates the most interesting business agenda that I think the law can offer to anyone today.

Kenneth MacRitchie

Lawyer, Projects

Kenneth MacRitchie is the Managing Partner of one of the largest US law firms in London. He has advised on some of the most complex and innovative structured finance transactions to have been completed in the London market, working with financial institutions and lending corporations on major financing transactions.

Recent projects include the development and financing of a $1.5 billion liquefied natural gas plant in Egypt, developing $1.6 billion financing of a Power Generation and Sea Water Desalination Plant in Abu Dhabi and developing the £1.26 billion financing of the London Underground.

He was the lead arranger of the £400 million financing for the new Wembley National Football Stadium.

For the lawyer like me who also lives for doing deals, there is no better place to practise than the City of London. It is endlessly exhilarating to work with highly talented individuals in all areas of business, all being stretched to put together the largest and most complex international business transactions.

Paul Maher

Corporate Lawyer, Vice-Chairman and Senior Partner

Paul Maher became a Senior Partner at Mayer Rowe Brown & Maw, one of the largest corporate law firms in the world barely thirteen years after joining and has recently become Vice-Chairman with primary responsibility for global strategy. The firm employs around 1500 lawyers across Europe, US and China.

Against a backdrop of conservative thinking in the cut-throat environment of corporate law, Paul has earned a considerable reputation for his innovative approach to case work as well as initiating a more communal ethos within his own firm.

I probably got into the law more by accident, some might say luck, than judgement. In fact, I was really interested in career writing although I wasn't really focused on how this would come to fruition. Anyway I did study law at University and accepted articles at a Westminster based law firm Boodle Hatfield. I spent six years in-house post qualification at ICI in London, which I enjoyed immensely. In 1990 I returned to private practice and joined Rowe & Maw. I have been lucky to be a practitioner at a time of tremendous transformational change in the markets generally but also in the legal services market place with even more seismic changes still to come.

Phil Michaels

Head of Legal, Friends of the Earth

Phil Michaels has been Friends of the Earth's in-house solicitor for the past five years. He was instrumental in forcing Gordon Brown, then Chancellor of the Exchequer, to reverse his decision to scrap environmental reporting for companies.

Last year he represented hundreds of cyclists who took part in the monthly 'Critical Mass' bike ride. The High Court duly found in the cyclists' favour, ruling that the Metropolitan Police had no right to treat the rides as a protest.

He also played a significant part in FoE's campaign to secure a judicial review of the Government's policy on genetically modified food and has also secured FoE's right to take legal aid cases, widening the number of people it can help.

On a good day the law really is capable of protecting those people and interests that are most in need of protection. Public interest lawyers, in whatever sphere, try to help the law to do this.

Ann Minogue

Lawyer, Construction

Ann Minogue has specialised in construction related contracts for real estate transactions for over twenty years. She has advised on the procurement routes and drafting of forms of contract for major developments, such as Broadgate, Paternoster, the Channel Tunnel and Spinningfields, Manchester.

She heads up the team responsible for construction work for Allied London, British Land, Heron and Stanhope development programmes, and has advised on construction work for the Royal Opera House, Tate Modern, Tate Britain, Royal Albert Hall, V&A Museum, Royal Shakespeare Company and other lottery funded arts projects

She is also a member of the Strategic Forum Olympic Task Group.

The respectability of law coupled with the buzz and glamour of property developments; the intellectual rigour of law coupled with the vision and inspiration of the big personalities of development. I drifted into it but it has kept me enthralled for the last 20 years.

Malcolm Nicholson

Lawyer, Competition

Malcolm Nicholson was educated at Cambridge and Brussels Universities and currently heads the Competition practice at one of the magic circle law firms.

He has dealt with obtaining regulatory clearance from the Merger Task Force of the European Commission for a number of high profile mergers and acquisitions, including both Phase II "serious doubts" cases, such as Guinness/Grand Metropolitan, and Phase I cases settled by undertakings, such as Unilever/Bestfoods and Glaxo Wellcome/SmithKline Beecham.

He has extensive experience before the OFT and the Competition Commission, including both merger and monopoly inquiries. He also has particular experience in utilities regulation, stemming from his involvement in the regulatory and competition aspects of privatisations, including gas, electricity and railways.

Start with a base of working alongside able and interesting business people over issues or transactions that matter; blend the business description and analysis with some transaction risk assessment; add a dash of industrial organisation economics and finally some law to blend it smoothly together … competition law is a heady cocktail.

Simon Oxley
Solicitor

W. Davies & Son was founded in 1909, as a general high-street practice and has been closely involved with the community of Woking ever since as honorary solicitor to Woking Chamber of Trade and Commerce since 1919 and has acted for Woking Hospice since the charity was formed. In the last few years, the practice has moved away from criminal work to specialise in commercial property, litigation and private client affairs.

Under new rules being considered in the Government's Legal Services Bill, non-lawyer ownership of firms would be permitted and the legal aid framework would change, making it more problematic for smaller firms to compete.

Supermarkets would be entitled to set up booths offering will writing and conveyancing; "cherry picking" the most the profitable work, which, it is feared, could lead to many high street firms facing closure.

So much change, so quickly! Solicitors must therefore embrace technological advance to the full; but above all solicitors must espouse virtue.

W. DAVIES
5

Gareth Peirce

Lawyer, Human Rights

Gareth Peirce is noted for taking on controversial cases, including high profile human rights issues. Her clients include the Birmingham Six, the Guildford Four, former MI5 operative David Shayler, and more recently, Abu Qatada, the family of Jean Charles de Menezes, Mozzam Begg and Bisher Amin Khalil al-Rawi, a detainee at the Guantanamo Bay detainment camp.

She was educated at Cheltenham Ladies' College and the University of Oxford and then moved to US, where she followed the campaign of Martin Luther King. She decided to return to Britain in the 1970s, and took a postgraduate law degree at the LSE and was admitted to the Roll of Solicitors in 1978.

Throughout the 1970s, Gareth Pierce campaigned for reform of the laws and police procedures that permitted the wrongful prosecution and conviction of persons solely on identification evidence.

We ought to have learned harsh lessons from our treatment in the 20th century of Irishmen and women suspected of involvement in terrorism when injustice in the name of the law served to fuel rather than prevent 30 years of conflict. Instead, it is a matter of bitter personal regret to observe since 2001 a chillingly similar abandonment of fundamental principles, domestically and internationally, this time in respect of a different community now made suspect, the Muslim community. Internment without trial, rendition, Guantanamo, the use of secret evidence and deportation to countries practicing torture should never have found a place in our vocabulary.

Inalienable rights exist to be enforced, not avoided or destroyed.

Tim Polglase

Lawyer, Banking

Tim Polglase advises on a range of structured finance transactions, but particularly domestic and cross-border leveraged buyouts, acting both on the initial transaction and on any subsequent restructurings. He led a team that advised on the first ever leveraged buy-out in Greece, involving the acquisition of a complany valued at Euro 1.6 billion.

A leveraged buyout occurs when a financial sponsor gains control of a majority of a target company's equity through the use of borrowed money or debt.

A leveraged buyout is a strategy involving the acquisition of another company using a significant amount of borrowed money to meet the cost of acquisition, typically 70% of the company's total capitalization, but it can reach as high as 95%.

The loan capital is usually borrowed through a combination of prepayable bank facilities and/or public or privately placed bonds, which may be classified as high-yield debt, also called junk bonds.

It's the application of the theory to the situation at hand which interests me. Although my tutor would be disappointed (but not, I suspect, entirely surprised) to hear it, the study of law as an academic subject did not grip me in the same way as I had enjoyed studying history. Using it in practice is a different thing, however – it is very stimulating applying what you know, in legal expertise and in market knowledge, to the transaction you are working on to deliver the result your client wants. An added bonus for me has been that as I have moved through my career the job has kept changing and challenging me. I am privileged to work in a firm of very capable and driven people and now have responsibilities not only to clients but also to the team in which I work, which has required me to focus on a different skill set.

Geraldine Proudler

Lawyer, Media and Defamation

For many years Geraldine has specialised in media litigation including defamation, breach of confidence, contempt of Court and broadcast complaint cases. She acts for national and regional newspapers, media and other companies, as well as managing the reputations of businessmen and high-profile individuals.

She acted for *The Guardian* in its successful defences against former cabinet minister Jonathan Aitken and Neil Hamilton MP in the 1990s as well as *The Sunday Mirror* and *Daily Mirror*. She was also involved in a case that produced one of the first High Court judgments in relation to alleged internet libel.

The days of a constant stream of libel trials in which politicians or other high profile claimants sued national newspapers have faded from memory. The lawyers who dealt with those cases now spend far more time dealing with damaging publications on the internet, closing down vexatious websites, tracing anonymous postings, and preventing the publication of confidential information or invasions of privacy on the web. The issues are more likely to be resolved with ISP's, Google, Microsoft or Facebook, and the new world is challenging, much faster moving, buzzy, interesting, and requires lawyers to have much quicker reflexes to adapt old legal tricks to new technology.

Fiona Shackleton

Lawyer, Family

Fiona Shackleton graduated in Law from Exeter University only taking up full time practice in 1980s, later becoming a partner at Farrer and Co, the royal solicitors.

Following her first high profile case, that of Prince Andrew and Sarah Ferguson, she went on to handle Prince Charles' divorce from Diana and has since represented Paul McCartney among other celebrities. She also acts as legal adviser to Prince William and Prince Harry.

Law started as a job for me, it has evolved into a career. It is only one of my faces, and by no means the most important one. Many of the skills used in the area I practice in have little to do with law and everything to do with wisdom, judgment and the understanding of people.

Robin Shaw

Lawyer, Media

One of Robin Shaw's most notorious clients is the popular satirical magazine, 'Private Eye' which is sued for libel on a regular basis and maintains a large quantity of money as a "fighting fund". Experience, however, has taught those behind the magazine various expiditious ways to defuse legal tensions. As editor, Ian Hislop has become one of the most-sued men in Britain.

Those who have sued the magazine include many famous names, and although politicians are a prime target, they tend to accept it, with the largest number of lawsuits being issued by journalists and businessmen.

The most famous litigation case against the magazine was initiated by the billionaire James Goldsmith, who managed to arrange for criminal libel charges to be brought. He sued over allegations that members of the Clermont Set, including Goldsmith, had conspired to shelter Lord Lucan The case threatened to bankrupt the magazine, which turned, succesfully, to its readers for financial support in the form of the Goldenballs Fund.

People who bring libel actions do not seem to realise (and presumably are not warned) that one of the effects of bringing a libel action (apart from getting an enormous bill) can be to generate a lot of publicity and press coverage about the very allegations they are complaining about and which they did not want published in the first place.

PRIVATE EYE
6

Jane Simpson

Lawyer, Family

Jane Simpson is the founder and head of a family law team and one of only a handful of women who heads a City of London law firm. She trained as a marriage guidance counsellor, and Collaborative lawyer and was co-founder of Resolution (formerly the Solicitors Family Law Association). She has served as a member of the Lord Chancellor's Family Law Advisory Board and was Vice Chairman of the Tavistock Portman NHS Trust.

Collaborative family law is a new, non-confrontational approach to resolving issues arising out of family or relationship breakdown. The collaborative process is based on discussions during which each client is supported by his/her own trained collaborative lawyer, without the threat of court proceedings, to find a mutually acceptable solution.

I have been lucky enough to have assembled and to lead one of the country's top family law teams, recognised widely for its quality, energy and commitment.

I like to think that, in very many of our cases, we really can make a difference, not only by resolving practical issues relating to children and money, but by helping our clients to deal with the trauma of divorce so that they are ready to rebuild their lives.

I am proud that the achievements of our team will continue long after I finish practising.

Clive Stafford Smith

Lawyer, Human Rights

Born in Suffolk, Clive decided to move to US and graduated from Columbia Law School in New York. He then spent nine years as a lawyer with the Southern Center for Human Rights working on death penalty cases and other civil rights issues.

In 1999 Clive founded Reprieve UK and, the following year, he was awarded an OBE for 'humanitarian services'.

Since 2004, he has focused on achieving due process for the prisoners being held by the US in Guantánamo Bay, as well as continuing his work on death penalty cases.

I am not sure I would call it a 'job'. It's a privilege to get up every morning and have the chance to bring a little power to the powerless, and just say no to governments who want to kill people, or hold them in endless darkness away from the rule of law. I only wish there were more hours in every day.

Tony Willis
Mediator

Before becoming an independent mediator in 1998, Tony Willis was head of a prestigious litigation practice in the City. He is now one of the country's most prominent commercial mediators having conducted more than 850 mediations as well as advising on dispute resolution mechanisms and solutions.

Mediations that he has been involved with have covered a wide variety of areas, from oil and gas to family trusts and inheritance. Clients have included multinational companies, individuals, as well as the Home Office, HM Revenue & Customs and Ministry of Defence.

Mediation offers a framework for opposing parties to come together to better understand each other's position in an attempt to settle differences without the need for expensive court proceedings.

Dialogue, negotiation and agreement are the best ways forward for anyone who values their future and their freedom on this fragile planet.

The mediator's tools are simple. Robust analysis, the great power of putting human beings face to face round a table, debate and much energetic shuttling between strongly held and strenuously argued points of view.

Rewarding beyond measure.

Barristers

Sir Crispin Agnew of Lochnaw Bt QC

Advocate, Scotland

Sir Crispin Hamlyn Agnew of Lochnaw, 11th Baronet QC, as well as being an Advocate, is an officer of arms, former explorer and Chief of the Name and Arms of Agnew.

As a major in the Royal Highland Fusiliers he took part in, and led, a number of expeditions to Everest, Antarctica, Patagonia and Greenland.

His heraldic career began in 1978 when he was appointed Slains Pursuivant of Arms to the Chief of the Name and Arms of Hay, the Earl of Erroll, Lord High Constable of Scotland. In 1986, he was appointed to the senior position of Rothesay Herald of Arms in Ordinary and he currently holds this position.

Since qualifying in 1982, he has acted for and advised local authorities, on education matters and he is on the panel of advocates retained by the Disability Rights Commission with a particular interest in special needs education. He is also held in high regard for his work in agricultural law.

Having come to the law from a historical perspective, I am very conscious that 'the law' defines the characteristics of a nation and how it perceives itself and empowers its citizens.

David Anderson QC

Barrister, EU Law

European Union law has evolved over the last thirty years as European member states have sought to take advantage of cooperation in a number of areas. The so-called 'three pillars' of the European Union represent the areas of the social and economic foundations of the EC single market, security and defense and lastly, Justice and Home Affairs.

One of the many challenges concerns the reconciliation of English Common law which has evolved over the centuries shaped by the outcomes of cases as they have arisen, with continental Civil law which is rooted in certain established legal principles.

European Union law aims – ambitiously – to provide both the ground rules for the peoples of our continent to live harmoniously together, and a framework for Europe to project itself to the outside world. For all its imperfections, it is the most advanced expression yet of the international rule of law. Trips to argue cases before the European Court of Justice in Luxembourg (and the European Court of Human Rights in Strasbourg) are testing, but often inspiring as well.

Monye Anyadike-Danes QC

Advocate, Northern Ireland

Monye Anyadike-Danes has over 20 years experience as a corporate and commercial lawyer. She was called to the Bar in 1980 and was subsequently called to the Bar of St Vincent and the Grenadines, the Bar of Northern Ireland and the Bar of the Republic of Ireland. She is a member of the Society of Construction law and the Chartered Institute of Arbitrators and is a Mediator.

She has lectured in business law and development issues and has acted as a consultant on development issues to the Commonwealth Development Corporation, North-South Institute and the UN Conference on Trade and Development (UNCTAD) and has presented at numerous conferences.

She moved to Northern Ireland in 1997 where has also developed a practice in Child and Family Law. In 2004 she was appointed Counsel to the Inquiry into Hyponatraemia-related Deaths established by the Department of Health, Social Services and Public Safety of Northern Ireland.

She was called to the Inner Bar in Northern Ireland in 2007, and is a member of the Bar Council sitting on a number of its Committees.

Sometimes it is not why you start but why you continue that is significant. For me it is because it has always been a privilege to act as someone's counsel in the law.

Michael J Beloff QC

Barrister

The Hon. Michael J Beloff QC, President of Trinity College, Oxford since 1996, was born in 1942 and educated at Eton and Magdalen College, Oxford. He was called to the Bar by Gray's Inn in 1967 and 'took Silk' as a Queen's Counsel in 1981 becoming a Member of the Court of Arbitration for Sport from 1996. He has served on the CAS ad hoc panel for dispute resolution for the Olympic and Commonwealth Games and on a special Arbitral panel for the FIFA.

He has presented cases before the House of Lords, European Court of Justice, European Court of Human Rights, and other Courts across the world.

'In the theatre of the law they also serve who only stand and speak.'

ADAPTED FROM MILTON

Nicholas Blake QC

Barrister

Pre-eminent in his field, Nicholas Blake has also written extensively on the subject of civil rights and in particular human rights in immigration and asylum law. His criminal experience includes acting in a number of celebrated miscarriage of justice cases and criminal trials including death penalty cases.

He has conducted cases in the Caribbean, Fiji, Hong Kong and has substantial experience before international tribunals, including the European Court of Human Rights, the European Court of Justice, the Inter American Commission of Human Rights and the Inter American Court of Human Rights.

As a law student Nicholas was one of the founders of the Free Representation Unit, and later became Chair of the Immigration Law Practitioners Association.

During my career public law has developed from its historic roots into a sophisticated instrument for holding the executive to account, supervising any excesses and ensuring effect is given to human rights principles. It is this supervision that is the basis for legitimate government. Chill winds may blow from time to time, but it has been constantly stimulating and a privilege to participate in this process.

John Creaney QC

Barrister, Northern Ireland

John Creaney was educated at Queen's University, Belfast and Trinity College, Dublin. He was called to the Bar in Belfast in 1957 and he is also a member of the Bar in Ireland, New South Wales and Cayman Islands.

The greater part of his work has been in the criminal courts. As Senior Crown Counsel during the 'troubles', he has prosecuted in many of the more serious 'terrorist' or Diplock (non jury) trials for over thirty years. He has also acted for the Serious Fraud Office in their fraud cases and for the Crown and Defence in jury trials.

My decision to pursue a career at the Bar was largely engendered by the exploits of the great Irish advocates, particularly Russell and Carson. When called in 1957 I found myself in a small, male dominated and conservative club. The criminal practitioner was regarded as eccentric: yet the 'craic' was good and friendships valued.

Fifty years later the Bar is vibrant, youthful with a discernable female influence. The advocate is much in demand, particularly in the criminal courts. The "craic" is still good and friendships still valued.

Barbara Dohmann QC

Barrister

As a QC of twenty years standing, Barbara Dohmann, who specialises in commercial law, has also acquired a vast amount of experience in many areas of the law including Banking, Insurance, Commercial Arbitration, Fraud, Company Law; Entertainment and Intellectual Property, International Law and Professional Negligence.

She was appointed in 2007 to be a part-time Commercial Judge of the Civil and Commercial Court at the Qatar Financial Centre in Doha and is a member of the Standard Committee of International Law ('the North Committee').

Both my parents were lawyers; they encouraged a love of language, logic and debate, and foremost a recognition that the good citizen fights for justice and individual liberty.

Donald Findlay QC

Advocate, Scotland

In order to practice as an Advocate in Scotland, one must join the Faculty of Advocates, which has been in existence since 1532 when the College of Justice was set up by Act of the Scots Parliament, but its origins are believed to predate even that event. Advocates are divided into groups, which are known as Stables of which there are twelve.

The Faculty is self-regulating, and the Court delegates to the Faculty the task of preparing Intrants for admission as Advocates. This task involves a process of examination and practical instruction known as devilling, during which Intrants receive intensive training in the skills of advocacy. No one can be presented to the Court as suitable to be a practising Advocate without satisfying these training requirements.

Donald Findlay is widely considered to be Scotland's premier advocate and has served as a defence lawyer in many high-profile murder cases including Jodi Jones, Mark Scott and the Kris Donald murder trials.

When someone is charged with a crime, they are entitled to be defended to the fullest extent allowed by law. After life itself, our personal liberty is the greatest gift we possess. It is better than 99 guilty men walk free than 1 innocent man be sent to jail. As a criminal lawyer and a believer in individual liberty, this has always been my guiding principle.

Lord Grabiner QC

Barrister, Commercial

Lord Grabiner is a leading commercial barrister with a substantial court and advisory practice dealing with the major commercial issues of the day. Highly experienced both as an advocate and an arbitrator in domestic and international arbitrations, he is a director of the London Court of International Arbitration.

He also sits as a Deputy High Court Judge of the Chancery and Queen's Bench Divisions and is a working peer in the House of Lords.

I love the independent professional lifestyle of being a self-employed advocate. I also get great satisfaction from achieving some sort of order out of the apparent chaos when the problem first arrived. For me it's the best job in the world.

Philip Havers QC

Barrister, Personal Injury

Educated at Eton & Cambridge, Philip Havers comes from an eminent legal family. His grandfather, Cecil Havers, rose to become a High Court judge, his aunt is Dame Butler-Sloss and his father, Michael Havers, rose further still to become Attorney General and then Lord Chancellor in 1987. His brother is the actor, Nigel Havers.

Philip Havers has a wide-ranging practice focused, in particular, on public law, human rights law, clinical negligence, health law, environmental law, personal injury law, breach of confidence and contempt of court.

He has appeared in many leading cases in these fields. One of these was the Diane Pretty case, pleading her right to an assisted suicide due to progressive motor neurone disease. The case went all the way to the European Court of Human Rights where it was finally turned down.

He is also an accredited mediator and Deputy High Court Judge.

'The business of the law is to make sense of the confusion of what we call human life-to reduce it to order but at the same time to give it possibility, scope, even dignity.'

ARCHIBALD MACLEISH, AMERICAN POET, 1892–1982

Christopher Jeans QC

Barrister, Employment

Before the Industrial Revolution, the average employee worked for around 12 hours a day, and with economic growth came even longer hours, with 16 hours not uncommon. Use of child labour was commonplace, often in factories, and women received far less wages than their male counterparts.

Times have changed, and in the past ten years there have been many changes in UK employment law. These include enhanced maternity and paternity rights, the introduction of a National Minimum Wage and the Working Time Directive which covers working time, rest breaks and the right to paid annual leave.

Discrimination law has also been tightened, with protection from discrimination now available on the grounds of age, religion or belief and sexual orientation as well as gender, race and disability.

Lyndon Johnson said that whilst law does not change society 'it points the way'. Employment and discrimination law has been pointing the way for three decades. Its basic tenet of fairness at work has been influential. Thirty years ago it removed separate wage scales for women and colour bars in clubs. Its onward march will render many of the practices of today unthinkable to the society of thirty years hence.

Baroness Helena Kennedy QC

Barrister, Crime

Helena Kennedy practises predominantly in criminal law, undertaking leading work of all kinds. She has undertaken judicial reviews, public inquiries and sex discrimination work, and has acted in many of the prominent cases of the last decade including the Brighton Bombing Trial and Guildford Four Appeal, the Bombing of the Israeli Embassy and the abduction of Baby Abbie Humphries.

She is Chair of the British Council and the Human Genetics Commission and is on the Advisory Council of the World Bank Institute. She has been a Labour Peer since 1997 and is a Bencher of Gray's Inn.

She is a frequent broadcaster and journalist on law and women's rights.

The law is the bedrock of a nation; it tells us who we are, what we value, who has power and who hasn't. It establishes the rules by which we live. And when we use it to translate human rights into reality and to secure justice, that is when the law becomes poetry.

Lord Lester of Herne Hill QC

Barrister, Human Rights

Anthony Lester was born in 1936 in north London. He went to Cambridge and Harvard and was called to the Bar in 1964 and became a QC in 1975. He sat as a Deputy High Court Judge before becoming a Liberal Democrat Peer in 1993.

He has campaigned tirelessly for more than thirty years to make the European Human Rights Convention directly enforceable in British courts and introduced two Private Members' Bills on the subject which became models for the Human Rights Act 1998.

He has also introduced Private Members' Bills, seeking to give the public direct rights of access to the Parliamentary Ombudsman and to give legal protection and recognition to unmarried couples (both same sex and opposite sex), and to modernise anti-discrimination legislation in a single Equality Bill.

Earlier this year, Lord Lester was appointed special advisor on constitutional reform to the Secretary of State for Justice.

'The spirit of liberty is the spirit which is not too sure that it is right'.

JUDGE LEARNED HAND

Ian Mill QC

Barrister, Media and Sport

Ian Mill is head of a well-known chambers in London and has built a reputation over the past few years in the areas of media and sport that is practically unsurpassed.

His client list from the world of music, which reads like a Who's Who, includes Michael Jackson, George Michael, U2, Spice Girls, Oasis, Eric Clapton, Elton John, Morrisey, Tom Jones, Andrew Lloyd Webber and the late Luciano Pavarotti.

No less impressive is his list of clients from the world of sport which includes the Football Association, the England and Wales Cricket Board, the Professional Golfers' Association, the Rugby Football Union, several Premier League football clubs, David Beckham, Tim Henman, Lennox Lewis, Mike Tyson and the Williams F1 racing team.

Sport and music have always been passions. To play a part, however peripheral, in these fields of activity is a privilege and a joy.

aigo
aigo
SAP
vodafone

Clare Montgomery QC

Barrister, Criminal law

Clare Montgomery is perhaps best known for her work on complex criminal cases. A QC of ten years standing, she has also developed a substantial and varied practice, having represented the Bar at the House of Lords, the liquidators of BCCI in a massive action against the Bank of England, as well as appearing for Sion Jenkins, whose conviction for the murder of his step-daughter was quashed in 2004.

Her most recent case involves the prosecution of the Metropolitan Police for its handling of events prior to the death of Jean Charles de Menezes, the wrongly identified suicide bomber.

To be asked to stand, as an advocate, between the subject and the Crown is an honour. The fact that what one advocates may contribute to maintaining the law as a pillar of freedom is a privilege. But above all advocacy is a pleasure; demanding and absorbing; full of human interest and intellectual rigour.

Gabriel Moss QC

Barrister, Insolvency

Gabriel Moss studied Jurisprudence at Oxford and went on to receive a Postgraduate Law Degree in 1972. He spent some years lecturing at the University of Connecticut Law School, then Oxford University and LSE.

He was appointed Queen's Counsel in 1989 and has specialised in insolvency ever since. He was the founding member of the Board of the Insolvency Research Unit, King's College, London, and a member of the Insolvency Committee of Justice at the International Commission of Jurists.

He was elected Fellow of the Society for Advanced Legal Studies in 1998 and has been a member of the Review Panel considering changes to English law in the light of the EU Insolvency Regulation since 2000.

Has written several leading texts on insolvency, reconstruction and rescue.

Legal specialists are sometimes described as people who learn more and more about less and less, but the most worthwhile specialist case I have dealt with was one in which we were able to safeguard the pensions of about a million people in every walk of life.

Nicholas Mostyn QC

Barrister, Family

Educated at Ampleforth and Bristol University, Nicholas Mostyn is one of the most eminent barristers in family law. He specialises in what is known as 'ancillary relief'.

English law looks upon the grounds for divorce and access to the children as the main issues, and resolving the financial issues as 'ancillary'. In practice, the main dispute in any divorce is often over the question of money, and that is very often the case when there are significant assets in dispute.

Nicholas Mostyn has represented many wives in high-value cases, among the most prominent, being Zoe Rowland, who claimed a share of her former husband's future inheritance worth a reputed £700 million.

He is currently acting on the other side for Paul McCartney whose estate is worth something in the region of £800m, in his divorce from Heather Mills.

In Act 2 of Die Walküre, *Fricka, the guardian of marriage demands and insists that her husband Wotan should severely punish the adulterous incestuous couple Siegmund and Sieglinde (who happen to be his children). Wotan resists, recognising no such thing as transgressive love, but eventually collapses, with disastrous results for all: a signal warning to those who would be overly damning of human failure within marriage. The consequences of breach of the marriage contract continue to have far reaching effects and their treatment by family professionals is, I suggest, as big a challenge as the law is capable of presenting.*

David Pannick QC

Barrister

Since his 'call to the Bar' in 1979, David Pannick has established himself as a leader in public, human rights, media, employment, sports and EU law.

He has argued over 75 cases in the House of Lords, more than 25 cases in the European Court of Justice in Luxembourg, and over 30 cases in the European Court of Human Rights in Strasbourg.

He has acted in many of the leading public law cases in the past 20 years, representing a wide range of clients including the Revd Moon, Chief Rabbi, Lord Chancellor, Mohammed Al-Fayed and Diana Princess of Wales.

He recently represented 'Liberty' in the House of Lords in the case which established that the detention without trial of terrorist suspects is a breach of the European Convention on Human Rights.

Mr Justice Jackson of the United States Supreme Court said in 1951 that as an advocate, he always had three arguments for any court appearance. 'First came the one that I planned – as I thought, logical, coherent, complete. Second was the one actually presented – interrupted, incoherent, disjointed, disappointing. The third was the utterly devastating argument that I thought of after going to bed that night.'

Judith Parker QC

Barrister, Family

An acknowledged leader in her field, Judith Parker practices in all areas of family law, particularly private child law. Her work deals with a myriad of sensitive issues including residence and contact disputes, education, sexual abuse, and international family law in relation to cross-border enforcement and international relocation.

Cases that she has taken have also dealt with parentage, surrogacy, assisted conception, and gender recognition.

She is a deputy High Court Judge in the Family Division as well as a regular lecturer on child law and related topics.

I have been a family lawyer since 1973.

What more could a practitioner want? Lots of law, lots of cross-examination, and every client with an interesting story to tell.

Gordon Pollock QC

Barrister, Corporate

Gordon Pollock heads one of the most profitable of all the barristers' chambers with its bias towards commercial litigation. Barristers are self-employed, and arrange themselves in groups known as chambers or sets, to share costs and help them win business.

In 1990 he was a key player following the insolvency of the International Tin Council which mushroomed in to a multi-national lawsuit of enormous complexity. He emerged having successfully fended off the claims of many powerful adversaries.

At around the same time he represented Lonrho following a protracted battle with the Government to release a report on its unsuccessful bid to acquire Harrods. The report was leaked and, as one consequence, the case was brought before the Law Lords, where Gordon Pollock pulled off the astonishing feat of persuading the judges to 'recuse', or disqualify, themselves from the hearing.

'The Worldly Hope men set their Hearts upon
Turns Ashes – or it prospers; and anon,
Like Snow upon the Desert's dusty Face
Lighting a little Hour or two – is gone.

And those who husbanded the Golden Grain,
And those who flung it to the Winds like Rain,
Alike to no such aureate Earth are turn'd
As, buried once, Men want dug up again.'

FROM 'THE RUBAIYAT', OMAR KHAYAM (1048–1131)

Rabinder Singh QC

Barrister, Human Rights

Since his call to the Bar in 1989, Rabinder Singh has become one of the most sought-after barristers in the fields of human rights and public law. He has represented clients in the House of Lords as well as the European Court of Human Rights and has also undertaken cases ranging from commercial and media to employment law.

In 2001 the Lawyer Magazine named him Barrister of the Year. A year later he was appointed QC, and in 2003 he was appointed Deputy High Court Judge, making him one of the youngest QC's and judges around. He is also a visiting Professor of Law at LSE.

Why did I become a barrister? The inspiration for me was a great but fictional lawyer called Atticus Finch in Harper Lee's novel 'To Kill a Mockingbird', gracefully played by Gregory Peck in the film version. Here was a lawyer presented for once not as a money-grabbing, word-twisting, logic-chopping hired gun but as a noble hero.

There is a moment in the story when a man spits in his face: just for a second Atticus flinches and nearly reacts with violence; then stops himself, gets out his handkerchief, wipes his face and quietly walks past him. He stays calm and keeps his dignity.

Jonathan Sumption QC

Barrister, Commercial

Educated at Eton and Oxford, Jonathan Sumption graduated in History with first class honours. He became a Fellow of History at Magdalen College, Oxford, before deciding to pursue a career in law. He was called to the bar in 1975, was subsequently appionted Queen's Council in 1986 and is now joint head of the country's highest earning chambers.

He is also a deputy High Court judge in the Chancery Division, and a judge of the Jersey and Guernsey Court of Appeal as well as being a member of the Judicial Appointments Commission and a Governor of the Royal Academy of Music.

He has also written extensively on medieval history, including a history of the Hundred Years' War in two volumes, shortly to be followed by a third.

There is no magic about the law. It is just common sense, with knobs on, plus a certain amount of articulate presentation.

Judiciary

Sir Peter Beaumont

Recorder of London

The most senior permanent judge at the Central Criminal Court, otherwise known as the Old Bailey, has the title of the Recorder of London, not to be confused with that of Recorder, which is the name given to lawyers who sit as part-time Crown Court judges.

The Central Criminal Court hears criminal cases from the capital as well as the most serious cases from around the country. The present Court building was built on the site of Newgate prison which used to hold public hangings right up until 1868. Court Number One is particularly atmospheric, having hosted the cases of Dr Crippen, the Krays and the Yorkshire Ripper, to name but a few.

It is a great privilege to serve as the 96th holder of an office stretching back in an unbroken line to Easter 1298.

Lord Bingham of Cornhill

Senior Law Lord

Born in 1933, Thomas Henry Bingham, now Baron Bingham of Cornhill, is one of the most senior judges in the country.

Following his tenure as Lord Chief Justice of England and Wales from 1996 to 2000, Lord Bingham moved to the House of Lords, the country's highest court of appeal, as the 'Senior' Law Lord.

He is a keen advocate of the reorganisation of the British court system, and under present Government proposals his title would become President of the Supreme Court, a new high court completely separated from the House of Lords.

'The judicial process will have approached perfection when the discussion between judge and lawyer is as free and natural as that between persons, mutually respecting each other, who try to explain their points of view for the common good. Such an arrangement would be a loss for forensic oratory but a gain for justice.'

PIERO CALAMANDREI, *EULOGY OF JUDGES*

His Honour Judge Jeff Blackett

Judge Advocate General

Following the introduction of a unified, standing army in the 17th century, the office of Judge Advocate General was created in order to regulate the professional conduct of English soldiers.

The office of the Judge Advocate General now deals with criminal trials of service men and women in the Navy, Army and Air Force for serious offences known as Courts-Martial. The JAG also oversees the judiciary, makes judicial appointments and will personally act as trial judge for the more sensitive and serious cases.

Judge Advocates are always civilians and preside over the conduct of Courts-Martial and rule on all legal matters arising, in a similar way to a Crown Court trial. They are appointed by the Lord Chancellor just as with District and Circuit Judges.

'General Melchett: The case before us is that of the Crown versus Captain Edmund Blackadder, alias the Flanders Pigeon Murderer. Oh, and hand me the black cap, will you – I'll be needing that.'

FROM *BLACKADDER GOES FORTH*

I wanted to set the record straight and place the Services Justice System on a par with the Civilian System – and we are getting there!

Sir Anthony Clarke QC

Master of the Rolls

The title of the office derives from the fact that originally, the office-holder was a clerk responsible for keeping the 'Rolls,' or records, of the Chancery court.

The Keeper or Master of the Rolls and Records of the Chancery of England, known as the Master of the Rolls, is the third most senior judge of England, the Lord Chancellor of Great Britain traditionally being first and the Lord Chief Justice second.

The Master of the Rolls is the presiding officer of the Civil Division of the Court of Appeal and is also responsible for registering solicitors, who are officers of the Supreme Court.

The law is not always such an ass as you think.

Rt Hon Lady Cosgrove

Judge, Scotland

Hazel Cosgrove studied Law at Glasgow University and was later admitted to the Faculty of Advocates in 1968. In 1979 she went on to serve as a Sheriff in Glasgow and then in Edinburgh until 1996, when she became the first woman to become a Judge of the Court of Session, Scotland's Supreme Court.

In 2004 she received an OBE for services to the criminal justice system in Scotland, and has also been awarded honorary degrees from a number of institutions.

She has recently retired as a Senator of the College of Justice but still sits on the bench occasionally when there is a shortage of judges.

The world depends on three things: Justice, Truth and Peace.

FROM THE TALMUD, (ETHICS OF THE FATHERS, 1:18)

The Hon Mr Justice Deeny

Puisne Judge, Northern Ireland

The judges and barons of the common law courts at Westminster, other than those having a distinct title, were called puisne judges. Following the Supreme Court of Judicature Act 1877, a 'puisne judge' came to signify a judge of the High Court other than the Lord Chancellor, the Lord Chief Justice of England, the Master of the Rolls or any head of Division.

The word puisne means 'junior' and is used to distinguish the ten High Court judges of N Ireland from senior judges sitting at the Court of Appeal.

Donnell Deeny was called to the Bar in 1974 and took silk in 1989. He is currently a member of the English Bar and Senior Council in the Republic of Ireland.

He is a former chairman of the Arts Council of N Ireland and a High Sheriff of Belfast.

Nor law nor duty made me judge,
Nor public men nor cheering crowds,
A lonely impulse of delight
Drove to this quiet in the court.
I balanced all, brought all to mind,
The years to come seemed waste of breath
Great use of breath the years behind
In balance with that life, this bench.

AFTER YEATS

Mrs Justice Dobbs

High Court Judge

Having spent her early years in Africa where her father ran his own legal firm, Linda Dobbs went to Edinburgh University, originally to study music but later switched to Russian and Law. She subsequently completed a Masters in Law and went on to complete a PhD in Soviet criminology and penology.

She was called to the Bar in 1981 and has since then published books and articles on road traffic law and specialised in white collar crime, Customs and Excise cases and serious sexual offences.

In 2006, following a brief spell as Chairman of the Criminal Bar Association, Linda Dobbs became Britain's first Black High Court judge.

Things are slowly changing and there are now ten women out of 108 High Court Judges, but a mere nine black circuit judges out of a total of 623.

Being a judge is about trying to do the right thing.

Rt Hon Lord Gill

Lord Justice Clerk, Scotland

As Lord Justice Clerk, Lord Gill is the second most senior Judge in Scotland, behind the Lord President of the Court of Session. He holds the title in both the supreme civil court – the Court of Session and the supreme criminal court – the High Court of Justiciary, and is in charge of the Second Division of Judges in the Court of Session.

In practice, the Lord Justice Clerk rarely presides at criminal trials in the High Court, with most of his time being spent hearing civil and criminal appeals.

Lord Gill trained as an advocate and was appointed Queen's Counsel in 1981.

In 2001 he was appointed Lord Justice Clerk following a seven-year tenure as Chairman of the Scottish Law Commission.

He is a Fellow of the Royal Society of Edinburgh and a Fellow of the Royal Scottish Academy of Music and Drama.

I have been a member of this profession for forty years. What a privilege it has been.

Justice Gloster

High Court Judge, Commercial Court

In 2006, after a period of years as one of the bar's top earners, Dame Elizabeth Gloster was appointed the first female judge of the Commercial Court.

The court oversees the country's largest cases and she joins a line-up of just ten female judges on the High Court bench, compared with ninety-seven male judges.

'Four things belong to a judge: to hear courteously, to answer wisely, to consider soberly, and to decide impartially.' (Attributed to Socrates)

I don't think I can improve on that.

Baroness Hale of Richmond

Lord of Appeal in Ordinary (Law Lord)

Born in Yorkshire, Brenda Hale studied law at Girton College, Cambridge, graduating top of her class. After becoming assistant lecturer in Law at the University of Manchester, she was called to the Bar in 1969.

Working part time as a barrister, she spent eighteen years working mostly in academia, finally becoming Professor of Law at Manchester in 1986. Two years earlier she had achieved the distinction of becoming the first woman and youngest person ever to be appointed to the Law Commission, overseeing a number of important reforms in family law during her nine years there.

In 1989 she was made a Queen's Counsel and a Recorder, and in 1994 became a judge in the Family Division of the High Court of Justice.

A decade on, she became only the second woman to be appointed to the Court of Appeal and in 2003 it was announced that she was to become the first female Lord of Appeal in Ordinary (Law Lord), and the following year was appointed life peer.

I went into the law not knowing what to expect but certainly not expecting to become a Law Professor or a Judge but have found the words of the judicial oath '... to do right to all manner of people, according to the laws and usages of this realm, without fear or favour, affection or ill-will' some of the most inspiring in the English language and, like all such inspirations, very difficult to live up to!

Lord Hamilton

Lord President and Lord Justice General, Scotland

The office of Lord Justice General is derived from the earliest monarch's first ministers, known as justiciars, and for a brief period in the 16th century the post was passed down through the Earls of Argyll.

Today, the Lord President is the head of the Court of Session, and as Lord Justice General, head of the High Court of Justiciary. He routinely presides in these courts dealing mainly with appeals. In addition to his judicial duties, the Lord President has general supervision over all the business of the Court of Session and the High Court, and is responsible for the policy governing these courts and the judges, and for the rules of court procedure.

He makes appointments to several Scottish tribunals and recommends appointments to Queen's Counsel. As the most senior judge in Scotland, the Lord President is routinely consulted on a wide range of matters concerning the law and the legal system, and he deals with communications and consultations with the heads of foreign and Commonwealth judiciaries.

'Law is the dictate of reason, determining every rational being to that which is congruous and convenient for the nature and condition thereof . . . .'

VISCOUNT STAIR, *INSTITUTIONS OF THE LAW OF SCOTLAND*

Sir Igor Judge

President of the Queen's Bench Division

Born in 1941 in Malta, Sir Igor Judge has enjoyed an eminent career as a barrister and judge.

Called to the bar in 1963, he became a Recorder in 1976 and took silk in 1979. He was appointed to the Queen's Bench Division in 1988 and to the Court of Appeal in 1996 and became the first President of the Queen's Bench Division in 2005 when that post was split from that of Lord Chief Justice.

The Queen's Bench Division as one of three divisions of the High Court, together with the Chancery Division and Family Division, contains the Divisional, Admiralty, Commercial and Technology and Construction Courts. It is largely concerned with cases of personal injury, negligence, breach of contract, libel and slander, non-payment of a debt, and possession of land or property.

ISABELLA: *'How would you be,*
If He, which is the top of judgement, should
But judge you as you are? O, think on that;
And mercy then will breathe within your lips . . .'

SHAKESPEARE, *MEASURE FOR MEASURE*

His Honour Judge Geoffrey Kamil

Circuit Judge

The 78 Crown Courts around the country deal with the more serious criminal cases such as murder, rape or robbery, some of which are on appeal or referred from Magistrates' courts.

Crown Court trials are heard by a Circuit Judge and a 12-person jury randomly selected from members of the public, with around 450,000 jurors selected every year.

Judge Kamil was born in Leeds and trained and worked for many years as a solicitor in Leeds Town Hall which until recently was the home of Leeds Crown Court.

The best piece of advice I have received, was given to me as a newly qualified solicitor, by my late senior partner Jack Levi, who was one of the finest solicitor advocates in the North of England and a legend in his lifetime. This was 'being a great advocate is to know when to bend the knee';.

Georgina Kent

Recorder

Becoming a Recorder is often the first step on the way to an appointment as a circuit judge. Recorders are drawn from the ranks of qualified solicitors and barristers who generally start out by sitting as part-time judges in the Crown Court. Their jurisdiction is similar to that of a circuit judge, but they will usually handle less complex or serious cases.

Recorders are required to manage cases as well as to determine claims at trial. A recorder's duties include assisting the parties to prepare for trial, presiding over court proceedings and delivering judgments in both applications and contested trials.

Life as a barrister is interesting and exciting with moments of frustration and exhaustion thrown in. Sitting as a Recorder has been challenging but rewarding. I feel privileged to have a part to play in one of the greatest legal systems in the world.

Sir Brian Kerr

Lord Chief Justice, Northern Ireland

Northern Ireland's legal system is similar to that of England and Wales with one main exception being that people accused of offences specified under emergency legislation, to deal with terrorism, are tried in the Crown Court without a jury.

In such cases, the prosecution must prove guilt beyond reasonable doubt and the judge has to set out in a written statement the reasons for conviction. There is an automatic right of appeal to the Court of Appeal against conviction and/or sentence on points of fact as well as of law.

Mr Justice Kerr, appointed Lord Chief Justice of NI in 2004, is the head of the judiciary, presiding over all the Courts of Northern Ireland.

It may be true, as H L Mencken said, that a judge is a law student who marks his own examination papers, but, happily, the test questions keep changing.

Lord Justice Sir Brian Leveson

Senior Presiding Judge for England and Wales

Born in Liverpool in 1949, Brian Leveson read law at Oxford and was called to the Bar at 21, the minimum allowable age. Returning to Liverpool, he built up his practice and gradually began prosecuting increasingly high profile cases across the whole of the north of England. He subsequently took Silk at just 37 years of age.

He began to spend more time in London involved in professional disciplinary work around corporate collapse and fraud such as Barings, the Maxwell group, BCCI and Poly Peck.

In 2000 he was appointed a Judge of the High Court, Queen's Bench Division and in 2006 he was appointed Lord Justice of Appeal when he was also appointed a Privy Councillor. He was finally appointed Senior Presiding Judge for England and Wales in January 2007, and, as such, is responsible to the Lord Chief Justice for the judicial operation of the Crown, County and Magistrates Courts throughout the country.

He sits in the Court of Appeal, presiding in the Criminal Division as well being a member of the Civil Division.

Central to the proper administration of justice in any society is an independent judiciary. Deciding those cases that come before us by doing 'right to all manner of people after the laws and usages of this Realm without fear or favour, affection or ill will' is the ultimate manifestation of that independence and we must strive to ensure that it is respected. We maintain this independence for the public as a whole and respect must extend from the legislature and the executive; without it, true freedom would be lost. This is at the core of what we do.

Lord Low of Dalston

Retired member of SENDIST

Colin Low was born in Edinburgh in 1942 and has been totally blind since the age of three. He was educated at Worcester College for the Blind, as well as Oxford and Cambridge Universities. He went on to teach Law and criminology at Leeds University, before moving to London in 1984 as Director of the Disability Resource Team. He joined the Special Education Needs and Disability Tribunal as a lay member in 1994.

SENDIST is just one of 27 Tribunals which are an important part of the justice system, handling more cases each year than the ordinary civil courts, many involving the most vulnerable people in our society.

In May 2006 Colin was appointed to the House of Lords as one of the seven new non-party-political peers. He has played a leading part in the campaigns for integrated education and for comprehensive disability rights and has had important roles in a wide range of organisations concerned with disability.

I have found the law a remarkably good basis for many of the things I have had to do: It fosters powers of analysis, encourages clear thinking and provides a good understanding of public administration, the machinery of government and the governance of organisations.

Mr Justin Philips

District Judge

Magistrates' Courts hear 95% of all cases brought before a court of law in this country and have been in existence for over 600 years resolving local disputes and keeping order in the community.

The Magistrates' Court is presided over by a tribunal consisting of three magistrates (Justices of the Peace) or by a District Judge and dispenses summary justice, under powers limited by statute.

Judge Philips, as District Judge, sits at one of two dedicated drugs courts set up in a pilot scheme by the Department for Constitutional Affairs in West London, achieving some notable success with his 'hands-on' approach compared with more conventional methods in dealing with drug offenders.

My judicial pupil master was the late John Nichols. He believed that the wonderful thing about the job was the ability to do good.

As the lead judge of London's first Drugs Court, I like to think that John is proud of his pupil's work.

Lord Phillips of Worth Matravers

Lord Chief Justice of England and Wales

The Lord Chief Justice of England and Wales was, historically, the second-highest judge of the Courts of England and Wales, after the Lord Chancellor. Although the Court of the King's (or Queen's) Bench had existed since 1234, the title of Chief Justice was not used until 1268.

Originally, each of the three high common law courts – the King's Bench, the Court of Common Pleas, and the Court of the Exchequer – had its own Chief Justice. The courts, however, were combined in 1875, leaving a single Chief Justice.

As a result of the Constitutional Reform Act 2005, which removed the judicial functions from the office of Lord Chancellor, the Lord Chief Justice is now the head of the judiciary in England and Wales.

'Not the King's crown, nor the deputed sword
The marshal's truncheon, nor the judge's robe
Become them with one half so good a grace
As mercy does.'

SHAKESPEARE, *MEASURE FOR MEASURE*

Nina Ruiz

Magistrate

Richard I appointed the first 'Keepers of the Peace' in 1195. Later on they become known as 'Justices of the Peace' and more recently 'magistrates'.

The 30,000 magistrates of England and Wales are all volunteers and come from various walks of life and do not usually have any legal qualifications. They undergo a training programme supervised by the Judicial Studies Board and are required to sit at least 26 times a year.

Ninety-five per cent of all criminal cases are dealt with by the Magistrates Court.

Sitting on my local bench is a humbling and rewarding experience.

Each day brings different people and stirs a variety of philosophical and emotional questioning: the diversity within my local community; the sadness of people's lives ruined by drug and alcohol addiction; the empathy for people who have tried and failed; but most of all, the hope that we, as local magistrates are helping to make a positive difference to society.

James Taylor

Sheriff Principal, Scotland

The office of Sheriff Principal has existed continuously since around the 11th century and until the 19th century there were 30 sheriffs principal. In 1975 Scotland was divided into six sheriffdoms, with each presided over by a full-time sheriff principal.

Located in the Gorbals district, Glasgow's Sheriff Court is reputed to be the busiest court in Europe presided over by the sheriff principal who divides his time between judicial and administrative duties which include appointments, miscellaneous advisory and consultative functions as well as ceremonial duties.

The court hears both civil and criminal cases.

What makes the practice of law fascinating, rewarding and challenging to me is the privilege of being invited to attempt to resolve other people's problems.

Robert Turner

Queen's Remembrancer

The Queen's Remembrancer is the oldest judicial post to remain in continual existence since the Middle Ages when, in 1164, King Henry II sent Richard of Ilchester to the Court of Exchequer to supervise the annual collection of taxes and 'put the King in remembrance of all things owing to the King'.

The Queen's Remembrancer as the last surviving member of the old Court of Exchequer is required to wear on top of his full bottomed wig, the black tricorn hat of the former Cursitor Baron (judge) of the Court of Exchequer and is also the Custodian of the Great Seal of Exchequer which is the seal of Office of the Chancellor of Exchequer but is placed in the care of the Remembrancer.

King Charles II in 1668 ordered the King's Remembrancer, Lord Fanshaw, to appoint Commissioners to supervise the planting and management of the timber in the Forest of Dean to ensure that the King had a good supply of timber in particular so as to provide an adequate supply of oak for building the ships of the Royal Navy. The Queen's Remembrancer still appoints Commissioners (16 in number) for this purpose.

The Office of the Queen's Remembrancer was created in 1164 at the time of the emergence of the Common Law which has been the foundation of our justice system ever since. As the oldest judicial office, the King's Remembrancer represents the concepts of development and evolution of a system of laws which the judges have found to be acceptable to the community as a whole. Evolution is always preferable to revolution and the preservation of such Offices as mine is an example of the strength of the Common Law which is at the heart of so many jurisdictions world wide.

Others

Elish Angiolini QC

Lord Advocate

Her Majesty's Advocate, also known as the Lord Advocate, is the chief legal officer of the Scottish Government and the Crown for both civil and criminal matters. As head of The Crown Office and Procurator Fiscal Service she is the chief public prosecutor for Scotland.

Dating back to 15th century, the Lord Advocate's role was redefined following Scottish devolution in 1999. Until quite recently, the Lord Advocate attended the weekly Scottish Cabinet meetings, but the current First Minister has ruled that the Lord Advocate should no longer attend the Scottish Cabinet in an attempt to 'de-politicise the post'.

Elish Angiolini is the first woman Procurator Fiscal, as well as being the first solicitor to be appointed to the post.

As Nelson Mandela has said, 'The test of our commitment to a culture of rights lies in our ability to respect the rights not only of the weakest but also of the worst among us'.

Sandra Bartlett

Wig maker

In 1635, the judges sitting at Westminster laid down Rules defining the different types of court dress which had evolved since the middle ages; rules that form the basis for much of the dress worn by High Court judges today.

It is Charles II, however, who is credited with the introduction of the wig, which gradually replaced the coif and skullcap, following his return from exile in France in 1680s.

Today the wig has become a vexed issue. Some argue that it alienates the public while others argue that the wig lends a necessary air of authority to a courtroom, particularly in criminal, as opposed to civil, cases.

The Full Bottom Wig. – Firstly, five head measurements are taken so that the correct wooden block may be chosen. This is then mounted and a net and silk ribbon trim is sewn on which acts as a base for the wig. The flaps are made and attached to the trim. Then woven horse hair is sewn on in rows. The top of the wig is frizzed out, as are the curls on the flaps which are then carefully put back in (see picture). Lastly, the wig is pressed with a hot iron enabling it to take on its finished look.

Martin Beard

Solicitor

Martin Beard has consistently volunteered his time and legal expertise at Centre 70, an Advice Centre in south London, over a period of many years. The centre provides advice for the local community on housing, welfare rights, employment, debt and consumer issues.

He is one of 2,000 solicitors who give advice at clinics around the country, helping around 26,000 people each year and covering every area of law apart from family law and immigration.

The pro bono (short for 'pro bono publico') movement goes back 30 years to the launch of the Free Representation Unit, which still provides young barristers, solicitors and trainees to represent clients at tribunals where there is no legal aid.

He has told you, O man, what is good;
And what does the LORD require of you
But to do justice, to love kindness,
And to walk humbly with your God? MICAH 6:8

At Trinity College I studied to be a lawyer and started also upon a higher calling. I decided years ago that the learning and skills I acquired in my legal work (as a partner at Dawson Cornwell and before with other London firms) could be used to help Centre 70 provide legal advice to the less well off. I've gained an incalculable wealth by the giving.

No.46
ESTATE AGENTS

Richard Cheesley

Tipstaff

The name 'Tipstaff' originates in the 14th century with the introduction of the first law enforcement officers who would apprehend a person intended for arrest with the aid of a *tipped staff*. The staff was made of wood or metal and topped with a crown, which was unscrewed to reveal a warrant of arrest inside the hollow staff. The modern day policeman's truncheon is a direct descendant.

The Tipstaff is the only person authorised to make an arrest within the precincts of the Royal Courts of Justice.

My job requires me to arrest and detain people wanted on warrant by the High Court and finding and removing children involved in Hague Convention Child Abduction matters. I meet many different types of people whilst carrying out my duties, although most of them are on the wrong end of the law, the job still provides me with a sense of achievement and a feeling that I have in some way made a difference to someone's life especially returning a child to a parent after they have been missing for some time.

Catherine Dyer

Procurator Fiscal, Scotland

Following a criminal investigation by the police (or other Specialist Reporting Agencies, e.g. Customs and Excise) a report is submitted to the local Procurator Fiscal, or public prosecutor.

The Procurator Fiscal then decides whether there is enough evidence to warrant criminal proceedings taking place, and subsequently he, or she, may decide to prosecute, offer an alternative to prosecution (such as a warning) or to take no further action.

In cases to be considered by a jury, the Procurator Fiscal will work closely with the police, interview witnesses and gather and review the forensic and other evidence and ultimately prepare the case for the court hearing.

'Salus populi suprema est lex' – The good of the people is the chief law.

CICERO, *DE LEGIBUS* III.iii.8

Dawn Elkin

List Officer

Fixing dates for trials involves the coordination of judges, clients, solicitors, witnesses, police and a myriad of support services. Once a trial date has been arranged, everyone is notified and the date confirmed, and in the case of civil hearings, a fee paid.

The Listing Office prepares the Daily List, which is the list of cases heard in the courts each day. It is an important part of the legal process, which allows the public to sit in on hearings, space permitting.

I have worked here at the Central Criminal Court since 1990 in a variety of posts. Initially I worked within the courtroom as usher and then a clerk which meant I was present during many high profile and fascinating cases.

My present role as List Officer is very exciting and challenging – balancing conflicting priorities such as witness and counsel's availability against the need to list cases as quickly as possible.

Sir Terence Etherton QC

Chairman of the Law Commission

The Law Commission was set up as an independent body in order to ensure that the law is as fair, modern, simple and cost-effective as possible. It achieves this through research and consultation with the best legal minds in the country making recommendations for consideration by Parliament. It also attempts to codify the law, eliminate anomalies, repeal obsolete and unnecessary enactments and reduce the number of statutes.

Many of the Commission's law reform recommendations have been implemented and it commands enormous respect from the international legal community due to the quality of its work and its independence.

The Law Commission was established in 1965 as a permanent independent body to keep under review the law of England and Wales with a view to its systematic development and reform. The political vision which inspired its creation was that the law should be accessible, intelligible and in accordance with modern needs. This is a vision which I feel privileged to serve.

WHO'S
WHO
2007
WOODFALL
LANDLORD
AND
TENANT

Michael Fordham QC

Barrister

Michael Fordham is a leading public law silk specialising in public law and human rights whose commitment to pro bono work has been publicly recognised.

Junior barristers and QCs volunteer their services through the Bar Council's pro bono unit, established by Lord Goldsmith, the former attorney general, which has just celebrated its 10th birthday.

Its recent successes include seeing off a threat to £50m of pension surpluses on behalf of pensioners, collecting a £230,000 award from the Criminal Injuries Compensation Authority for a builder and representing a nurse who successfully fought disciplinary charges threatening her livelihood.

Lawyers who worked without fee last year include the solicitors who stepped in to help the victims of the July 7 London bombings. Some manned hotlines giving advice on issues from insurance to death certificates, while 43 law firms prepared claims to the Criminal Injuries Compensation Authority.

The hymn-writer F. Pratt Green's hardest-hitting verse begins 'Across the world, across the street, the victims of injustice cry.' Perhaps the most important part of our job as lawyers is to cross the street, to try to communicate that cry to judges and ask that justice be done.

Professor Dame Hazel Genn QC

Professor of Socio-Legal Studies

Hazel Genn is Professor of Socio-Legal Studies at University College London, where she is also an Honorary Fellow. She is a leading authority on civil justice and has published widely in the field.

Her work has focused on the experiences of ordinary people caught up in legal problems and the responsiveness of the justice system to the needs of citizens. Her work has had a major influence on policy-makers around the world and she is regularly invited to lecture and provide advice abroad.

In January 2006, she was appointed an Inaugural Commissioner of the new Judicial Appointments Commission established under the Constitutional Reform Act 2005 and has been a member of the Committee on Standards in Public Life since 2003.

My approach to the study of law comes from the dual perspectives of law and social science. Interested in how law works in the real world, my career has been devoted to understanding the reality of law in action – listening to the experiences of the public caught up in legal disputes and studying how lawyers and judges do their jobs. The attraction for me comes from the importance of law in society and its contribution to stability and social justice. I cannot imagine ever exhausting my fascination with the day-to-day reality of the justice system.

Susan Hemming

Counter-Terrorism, CPS

Susan Hemming was called to the Bar in 1988 and worked for the Crown Prosecution Service in Cambridgeshire until 2000 when she moved to the Casework Directorate in London. Her current post as Head of Counter-Terrorism deals with all terrorism prosecutions in England and Wales.

Counter-Terrorism is one of the most demanding areas of the CPS' workload due to the public and political pressures to prevent loss of life on a potentially large scale. There are calls for the tightening of laws including the proposed increased detention periods for suspected terrorists, which have to be weighed against the erosion of civil liberties.

So far, in 2007, 37 people have been convicted in the courts of terrorist offences of which 15 pleaded guilty.

I first joined the CPS from pupillage as I wanted to get advocacy experience quickly. Initially I intended to go back to the Bar, but made the CPS my career after discovering that it was far more challenging to build a prosecution case than to pull one apart! Little did I know that one day I would get the opportunity to work with some of the best investigators in the world to build the most challenging and rewarding cases of all; against international terrorists.

Andrew Holroyd

President of The Law Society

In 1823, several prominent solicitors came together to form 'The London Law Institution' in an attempt to raise the reputation of the profession by setting standards and ensuring good practice. Two years later The Law Society came into being under the title of 'The Society of Attorneys, Solicitors, Proctors and others not being Barristers, practising in the Courts of Law and Equity of the United Kingdom'.

Women were not admitted as solicitors until 1922, but today account for more than half the admissions to the profession.

The Law Society, apart from representing over 130,000 solicitors in England and Wales, aims to influence the development of law and procedure through campaigning and lobbying.

It is a privilege to be leader of the Solicitors profession which includes amongst its members, on the one hand, the largest law firms in the world contributing hugely to our national economy and the success of global business and, on the other, lawyers who battle for the rights of the poor and the most marginalized citizens in our community. It is in our diversity that we find our strength.

Emma Hunt

Chair, Northern Ireland Young Solicitors Association

Emma Hunt graduated in Law from Queens University Belfast and subsequently completed a Master's Degree in Commercial Law at University College Dublin.

Since joining the Belfast law firm, Mills Selig, in 2001, she has been involved in many areas of litigation. She advises on land and property disputes as well as Criminal Damage applications and appeals. She has also worked as part of a team on major defamation actions and forensic investigations and has represented a large number of clients in tribunal cases and regularly advises on corporate transactions.

After three years as a member of the Northern Ireland Young Solicitor's Association, she was appointed to the position of Chair in 2006.

In the few short years of my career to date, I have learned that it is destined to be one of infinite variety. The skills of handling day to day legal work sit alongside the ever-present challenge of keeping up-to-date. Alongside that, my role as Chair of the Northern Ireland Young Solicitors Association opened up to me the people and legal systems of other countries worldwide: the similarities and at times, the stark differences. The learning curve will never end – this is truly a multidimensional career!

Professor David Ibbetson

Regius Professor of Civil Law

Regius Professorships were introduced to the universities of the time by various monarchs throughtout the middle ages in order to inroduce a measure of stability and control over these powerful institutions. In theory, the holder of the chair is still chosen by The Crown, although in practice the monarch acts on advice from a group of eminent peers.

The Regius Professorship of Civil Law is one of the oldest and most prestigious of the professorships at the University of Cambridge, founded by Henry VIII in 1540, with a princely sum of £40 per year attached.

Law is the most enthralling subject to study and teach – science and art, immensely stable through time with the capacity to adapt to change, moral philosophy coupled with hard-edged realism, the protector of individual freedom with the potential to become the tool of intolerable oppression.

Terry Johnson

Patent and Trade Mark Attorney

Patent Attorneys generally come from a scientific background and Terry Johnson is no exception, having graduated in Metallurgy and Materials Science. He is also a Trade Mark Attorney, advising clients on the registration, use and exploitation of their trade marks, both in the UK and worldwide.

He started out at the UK Patent Office as an Examiner, where for three years he examined patent applications in the metallurgical, materials science, and plastics moulding fields. He then moved to a leading firm of patent attorneys who then merged with Marks & Clerk, who have been established for more than 100 years, where he is now a Partner.

Terry has a wealth of experience in advising major UK and international clients on patents in a range of fields including building components, the water industry, LCD flat screens, and the handling of powder flow technology.

He is a regular lecturer worldwide on intellectual property and he was recently elected a Member of Honour by FICPI, the international body representing patent attorneys.

Intellectual Property Law, which is what I practice as a Patent Attorney, is practically a hobby for me in that its pursuit on behalf of a client's business gives me both endless pleasure and intellectual stimulation.

Tim Lawson-Cruttenden

Solicitor-Advocate

Since the Courts and Legal Services Act 1990, it has been possible for solicitors to qualify to appear before the Higher Courts, something previously denied them. Tim Lawson-Cruttenden is an enthusiastic solicitor-advocate who regularly appears at the High Court. He has also appeared in the Court of Appeal on harassment matters.

Tim was commissioned in the Blues and Royals during his gap year and served as an officer in the British Army. After serving as an officer he went to Sydney Sussex College, Cambridge where he read History and Law.

Since qualifying as a solicitor in 1979 he enjoyed a wide variety of casework, and at one point was representing the Sex Pistols in all their glory. He has since specialised in harassment law, helping the victims of stalking or domestic violence as well as victims of animal-rights extremists.

'To act justly and to love mercy and to walk humbly with your God.'

MICAH 6:8

– Words which never fail to inspire me but which are difficult to live up to.

Sir Ken Macdonald QC

Director of Public Prosecutions

By the middle of the 19th century, professional Police Forces had only just begun to emerge and people had to find their own lawyers or present the prosecution case themselves. In 1880 the Home Office appointed the first Director of Public Prosecutions who originally dealt only with a small number of important or difficult cases and once the decision to prosecute had been taken the handling of the prosecution was taken over by the Treasury Solicitor.

The police continued to have responsibility for most prosecutions right up until 1986, when the Crown Prosecution Service was finally installed with the DPP at its helm.

The DPP nowadays is responsible for ensuring the independent review and prosecution of criminal proceedings started by the police in England and Wales. He also makes decisions about the most complex and sensitive cases that arise.

'Our defence is not in our armaments, nor in science, nor in going underground. Our defence is in law and order'.

ALBERT EINSTEIN

Noelle McGrenera QC

Chair of the Bar Council, Northern Ireland

A student of Queen's University, Belfast, Noelle McGrenera was called to the Bar of Northern Ireland in 1978 and took Silk in 1999. A Deputy County Court Judge since 1993, she was appointed a Bencher of The Inn of Court of Northern Ireland in 2003 and has served on the Bar's governing bodies over many years. She has chaired various Committees of the Bar including the Equal Opportunities Committee and the Family Bar Association. She is currently Co-Chair of the International Council for Barristers and Advocates and of the Forum for Barristers and Advocates within the International Bar Association. She is also a member of the Bar of Ireland.

She has represented the Bar of Northern Ireland all over the world and will be co-hosting the World Conference of Advocates and Barristers to be held in Belfast and Dublin in June 2008.

She is currently practising in Family, Civil, Employment, Discrimination and Human Rights Law. She is a member of the Senior Civil Crown Panel.

She has appeared on many occasions in the Court of Appeal in Northern Ireland, in the European Court of Justice in Luxembourg and in the House of Lords.

When I was called to the Bar of Northern Ireland in 1978, female barristers were very much the exception.

Today, as the first women elected to lead our Bar, I am confident that the Bar of Northern Ireland values diversity and that the continued involvement of women at all levels in the profession is assured.

Joshua Rozenberg

Legal Correspondent

Joshua Rozenberg is Britain's best-known commentator on the law. He was the BBC's legal correspondent for 15 years before moving in 2000 to the *Daily Telegraph*, where he continues to write a weekly column as the newspaper's legal editor.

Because he trained as a lawyer before becoming a journalist, he is often the first port of call for broadcasters faced with a breaking legal story. Well respected by lawyers and the judiciary, he is frequently asked to chair or address legal conferences and other events. Joshua launched the popular BBC series *Law in Action* as its first presenter.

He holds an honorary doctorate in law from the University of Hertfordshire and is an Honorary Bencher of Gray's Inn.

'This is such an appalling vista that every sensible person in the land would say: "It cannot be right that these actions should go any further."' (Lord Denning, Master of the Rolls, 1980, explaining why he had blocked attempts by the Birmingham Six to prove they had been convicted of 21 murders on perjured police evidence). The six were cleared more than a decade later.

Pamela Sanderson

Court Clerk, Old Bailey

The most visible of the Court Clerk's in-Court duties are arraignments (asking defendants if they are pleading guilty or not guilty), swearing in Juries and taking verdicts at the conclusion of a trial. Less noticeable are the preparation of Judge's papers in advance of all hearings, keeping an events log of happenings in Court, and ensuring the smooth running of the Courtroom. The Court Clerk is also the conduit between Courtroom users and the Judge.

Outside the Courtroom The Court Clerk is responsible for the paperwork, Imprisonment Warrants, Community Orders, Bail Forms and, in recent times, the supervision of the electronic equipment The Clerk's benches these days make good use of computers as well as video link equipment allowing every Courtroom at the Old Bailey to link up with anywhere in the world.

Upon joining the Courts 25 years ago, a colleague told me that I would experience the full range of human emotions – except boredom. So far she has been right.

Court listings are predictable, the cases are not. On any day the balance can change instantly from a variety of sources. Clerks are advised to emulate the swan and glide smoothly over the surface with legs paddling furiously beneath.

It is a privilege to work in the flagship Crown Court, made doubly so by being clerk to the Recorder of London.

Baroness Scotland QC

Attorney General

The office of the Attorney General originated in 14th century when the Crown began to appoint a 'King's Attorney' to prosecute its business in the Court of Common Pleas.

The Attorney General in more recent times has evolved to become the Government's chief legal adviser as well as being responsible for overseeing the work of the Crown Prosecution Service and the Serious Fraud Office and in Northern Ireland they superintend the functions of the Director of Public Prosecutions.

Patricia Scotland was called to the Bar in 1977 and received Silk in 1991. She then joined the Foreign and Commonwealth Office in 1999 as Parliamentary Under-Secretary before moving to the Lord Chancellor's Department followed by a move to the Home Office.

Baroness Scotland was appointed Attorney General in 2007.

The law, thank God, gives everyone a voice.

Paul Shrubsall

Senior Barristers' Clerk

Barristers' clerks deal with the day-to-day administration in barristers' offices (known as chambers), and organise the workload of the barristers working there.

Senior barristers' clerks (also known as chambers directors or practice managers) have much influence in chambers. They are responsible for bringing business into chambers, allocating cases to barristers, negotiating fees, financial management of the chambers and recruiting, training and supervising junior clerks.

'Lovel took care of everything. He was at once his clerk, his good servant, his dresser, his friend, his "flapper", his guide, stopwatch, auditor, treasurer. He did nothing without consulting Lovel, or failed in anything without and expecting and fearing his admonishing. He put himself almost too much in his hands, had they not been the purest in the World. He resigned his title almost to respect as a master, if Lovell could ever have forgotten for a moment that he was a servant'.

CHARLES LAMB, ESSAYIST (1775–1834)

Michael SULLIVAN
Anthony de GARR ROBINSON
Neil KITCHENER
Alain CHOO CHOY
Hannah BROWN
David WOLFSON
David CAVENDER
David TOLEDANO
Daniel SULLIVAN
Zoe O'SULLIVAN
Emma HIMSWORTH
Edmund NOURSE
Graeme HALKERSTON
Saad HOSSAIN
Camilla BINGHAM
Philip ROBERTS
Michael FEALY
Orlando GLEDHILL
Simon COLTON
Matthew COOK
Steven ELLIOTT
Guy HOLLINGWORTH
Ben STRONG
Derek SPITZ
Anna BOASE
James GOLDSMITH
James NADIN
Daniel HUBBARD
Richard BOULTON
Michelle MENASHY
Conall PATTON
Laurence EMMETT
Henry FORBES SMITH

Brian Sloan

Law Student

Law has been studied and taught in Cambridge since the thirteenth century, when the core subjects of legal study in all European universities were Civil law (the law of ancient Rome) and the Canon law of the Church. Early graduates of the Cambridge Faculty of Canon Law held the highest judicial positions in Europe at the Rota at Avignon.

The student body, which is one of the largest law schools in the country, comprises nearly 740 undergraduate and 250 graduate students. Cambridge judicial alumni include a former President as well as a current member of the International Court of Justice, two former judges of the European Court of Justice, and several members of the Appellate Committee of the House of Lords and of the Court of Appeal.

Law provided the perfect solution to my problem of what to study at university, since it encompassed most of my interests, including history, politics and ethics, and is applied in practice on a daily basis. The law touches the lives of everyone, and at its heart lie questions of right and wrong – the most fundamental questions of all.

Jack Straw

Lord Chancellor and Secretary of State for Justice

In 2003 the Government announced its intention to create a Supreme Court, thereby separating the highest appeal court from the House of Lords and removing the Lords of Appeal in Ordinary from the legislature.

As part of that process a new position of Secretary of State for Justice was created in 2007 to replace the Secretary of State for Constitutional Affairs, which was originally intended to fulfill functions of the office of Lord Chancellor.

At the same time, the Department for Constitutional Affairs was abolished, and a Ministry of Justice was created in its place, taking over responsibility for sentencing policy, probation, prisons and prevention of re-offending.

Jack Straw originally trained as a barrister and later became special adviser to Barbara Castle and Peter Shore. He then worked as a researcher for Granada Television's *World in Action* programme before joining the Labour shadow cabinet. He was recently appointed the first Secretary of State for Justice following four years as Home Secretary and five as Foreign Secretary in Tony Blair's Labour cabinet.

I went into the law because I was attracted to the challenge both personal and intellectual. Personal, because no one else from my family had ever done so; intellectual, because I thought it would keep my brain cells active. So it has proved, though after a rather longer interlude in politics than I had anticipated, here I am as the Lord Chancellor.

Janet Thomas

Court Usher

Court ushers work under the direction of the Court Clerks in County and Crown Courts. Their responsibilities include preparing courtrooms, swearing-in witnesses and jurors, maintaining order in the court, passing messages between the court clerk and the lawyers, acting as Jury Bailiff when the jury retires to consider its verdict, and finally clearing up the court or chambers at the end of a session.

It can be a daunting experience for a juror, new to criminal proceedings to have to listen to evidence for long periods of time and finally make a decision that could have serious consequences for the defendant, and it is the Court usher whose responsibility it is to guide the juror through that process.

After doing Jury service, I was extremely lucky to be employed as an usher, a post I have held for 17 years. The Central Criminal Court, the cases the people are unrivalled in variety. No other job compares.

My role as an Usher is front-line, to meet and greet all Court users, in particular Jurors, they are members of the public unfamiliar with Court business, they need reassurance from a friendly face.

Geoffrey Vos QC

Chairman of the General Council of the Bar of England and Wales

The General Council of the Bar (known as the Bar Council) was founded in 1894 with the aim of improving the services and functions of the Bar, and representing the interests of the Bar on all matters relating to the profession.

The current Chairman, Geoffrey Vos, is also Head of Chambers and sits as a Deputy High Court Judge in the Chancery Division and as an arbitrator, mainly in insurance and reinsurance matters. He has been involved in litigation in a wide variety of fields including cases such as Apple Music v. Apple Computer, the Estate of Francis Bacon, Director General of Fair Trading v. Premier League BBC and BskyB, Maxwell and Barings.

Lawyers serve the public interest. To do so successfully, they need to command the confidence of the clients they represent. Such confidence is much enhanced if entry to the profession is accessible to people from all economic and ethnic backgrounds, and if the profession provides a demonstrably excellent service. We must strive to achieve these objectives in order to become truly representative of all sections of society.

3
3

Lord Woolf of Barnes

Lord Chief Justice of England and Wales, retired 2005

Harry Woolf was born in Newcastle upon Tyne in 1933. He studied law at University College London and was called to the Bar in 1955. Following a spell as First Treasury Counsel, he was appointed as a High Court judge. In 1992 he was created a life peer, as Baron Woolf, following his appointment as a Law Lord, becoming Master of the Rolls four years later, until 2000, when he was apppointed Lord Chief Justice.

He was an outspoken critic of the Constitutional Reform Act, which will create a Supreme Court to replace the House of Lords as the final court of appeal. He was also the head of the committee that reformed civil law in an attempt to make it more accessible. The Civil Procedure Rules 1998, are a direct result of his work.

He is a keen supporter of prison reform and in 1991 produced the 'Woolf Report', regarded by many as the most enlightened blueprint for improving the prison system in the last fifty years.

People should be prepared to stand up for justice.